Tales, Treasures and Pirates

of Old Monterey

Randall A. Reinstedt

Ghost Town Publications
Carmel, California

If bookstores in your area do not carry *Tales, Treasures and Pirates of Old Monterey*, copies may be obtained by writing to . . .

GHOST TOWN PUBLICATIONS
P.O. Drawer 5998
Carmel, CA 93921

Other books by Randall A. Reinstedt, offered by Ghost Town Publications, are:

GHOSTS, BANDITS AND LEGENDS of Old Monterey
MONTEREY'S MOTHER LODE
SHIPWRECKS AND SEA MONSTERS of California's Central Coast
GHOSTLY TALES AND MYSTERIOUS HAPPENINGS of Old Monterey
WHERE HAVE ALL THE SARDINES GONE?
MYSTERIOUS SEA MONSTERS of California's Central Coast
INCREDIBLE GHOSTS of Old Monterey's HOTEL DEL MONTE
INCREDIBLE GHOSTS of the BIG SUR COAST
GHOST NOTES

Also available by Randall A. Reinstedt is the **History & Happenings of California Series** . . . putting the *story* back in hi*story* for young readers.

10 9 8 7 6

Manufactured in the United States of America

Library of Congress Catalog Number: 79-110354
ISBN 0-933818-03-3

Cover and map illustrations by Tony Hrusa

INTRODUCTION

onterey – a gem in Spain's old world crown – is a city steeped in tradition and romantically linked to the colorful history of the vast California territory. Even though her rounded bay was first spotted in 1542 by the Portuguese navigator Juan Rodriquez Cabrillo (who sailed under the flag of Spain), Monterey's shores remained untrodden by visitors from distant lands until the English privateer Francis Drake – as documented by an aged plate of lead – dropped anchor here in 1579. In 1602 the Spanish explorer Sebastian Vizcaino became enamored with the beauty, the setting, and the potential of the great natural harbor, and blessed the Alta California bay with the name Monterey. It was here – two centuries ago – that Father Serra lived and died, and oversaw the beginning of California's famed Mission Period. It was the picturesque village of Monterey that Spain and Mexico chose for their capital city. It was Monterey that was attacked and sacked by a bold Pacific pirate over a century and a half ago. The infamous bandit Tiburcio Vasquez called Monterey his home, and it was here that he was born in 1835. It was Monterey that was taken over by the United States in 1842 – only to be given back to Mexico two days later. In 1850 the blustery Constitutional Convention was staged in old Monterey – paving the way for California to become a state. Nearly one century ago it was here that Robert Louis Stevenson found himself, his love and, what many believe, his literary career. The list is as endless as is the history of the West. Monterey, California's village by the bay, was founded before America became a nation, and her colorful background makes her one of the most history-rich communities in the western United States.

   With such a vast and varied background it seems little wonder that Monterey's history lends itself to a book of this type. "Tales, Treasures and Pirates of old Monterey" is, in a sense, a continuation of the books "Ghosts, Bandits and Legends of old Monterey", "Monterey's Mother Lode", "Shipwrecks and Sea Monsters of California's Central Coast", and "Ghostly Tales and Mysterious Happenings of old Monterey", all by Monterey-born historian Randall A. Reinstedt. These books revolve around the remarkable history of the Monterey Bay area, and these books, in their own way, tell different stories and offer varied glimpses into Monterey's multi-sided

3

personality. With "Tales, Treasures and Pirates of old Monterey" bringing to the front several previously untold tales, and documenting several unrecorded treasures, as well as vividly describing her involvement with Pacific pirates and attacks from the sea, it is hoped by the author that the book will fill a void and help to bring to the public a more complete picture of the varied, the unusual, the romantic, and the little-known happenings of long ago that have helped to make the Monterey Bay area the historically rich area that it is.

One of the many twenty-dollar gold pieces found in Monterey's century-late rush for gold. Yet to be cleaned, the coin appears as it did when it came out of the ground. See story and additional illustrations beginning on page 45. Credit — R.A. Reinstedt Collection.

ACKNOWLEDGEMENTS

Without the help of countless individuals, "Tales, Treasures and Pirates of old Monterey" could not have been written. It is to these people that this book is dedicated. Hopefully, through the publication of this work, their stories, their interests, their generosity and their experiences will live on.

In continuing, the author wishes to state that it would be most difficult to individually acknowledge each person who has had a part in bringing this book to completion, simply because the list is nearly endless. However, he also feels it would be extremely unjust to publish the book without acknowledging a chosen few.

The late Daniel Ross Martin is one such individual. Without the notes of this pioneer resident (born in the south coast's picturesque Palo Colorado Canyon in 1859), portions of this narrative would not have been included.

Mike Maiorana, the lad who found thirty-seven twenty-dollar gold pieces in Monterey's century-late rush for gold, added a touch of authenticity to this tale of treasure that only he could have contributed.

Mrs. Ruby Woicekowski, daughter of the late Al Geer, and present when Alfred K. Clark told his tale of Big Sur's mysterious underground world, kindly loaned her photographs and reminisced about Uncle Al and his lonely life.

Charles Krenkel and the late Adrian Harbolt, descendents of true Los Burros pioneers, talked of the historic days of gold mining in Monterey County and unselfishly shared many valuable memories.

Harry Downie, curator and restorer of beautiful Carmel Mission, added considerable information and aided in the research of several treasure tales. An example is the story of the Sanchez treasure. Without the use of Harry's personal file, and the carefully researched account of the events surrounding this tale contained therein (by the late historian Helen Wells), the intriguing story of Monterey's lost $85,000.00 treasure would not be as accurate as it is.

Don Howard, noted archaeologist and President of the Monterey County Archaeological Society, shared his knowledge, gave of his time, and willingly helped track down lost mines and forgotten cabin sites.

The late Mrs. Myron Oliver, wife of the man who succeeded in extracting the Drake scroll from the aged bottle, and a witness to the scroll having been in the bottle, graciously hosted the author one afternoon, helping to clear up clouded facts concerning this interesting chapter in Monterey history.

The above names list only a token few of the many people who actively helped with the research of this book. Without their help, the help of countless other individuals, and without the vast amount of information gleaned from yellowed newspapers, musty books, and aged diaries, the writing of "Tales, Treasures and Pirates of old Monterey" would not have been possible.

With this in mind, and with a tip of the hat to all the research librarians in the area, as well as to Jessie Sandholdt, Mary Sherman and Debbie and Erick Reinstedt, the author wishes to extend his sincere thanks to all concerned.

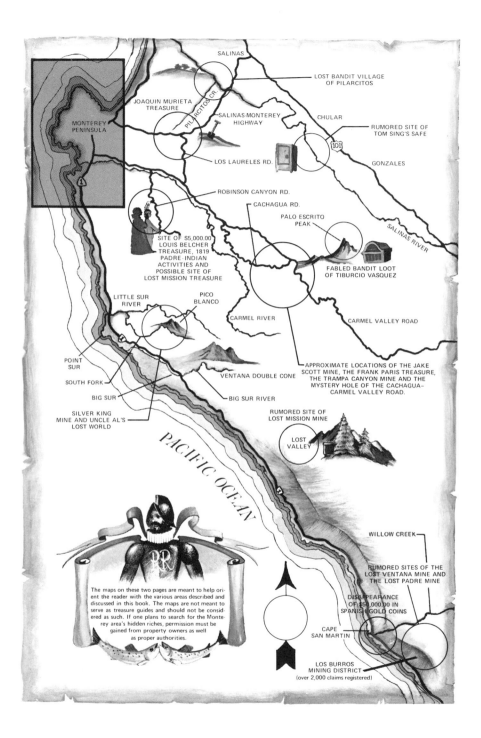

SALINAS

LOST BANDIT VILLAGE
OF PILARCITOS

JOAQUIN MURIETA
TREASURE

SALINAS-MONTEREY
HIGHWAY

CHULAR

PILARCITOS CR.

MONTEREY
PENINSULA

RUMORED SITE OF
TOM SING'S SAFE

101

LOS LAURELES RD.

GONZALES

ROBINSON CANYON RD.

CACHAGUA RD.

PALO ESCRITO
PEAK

SALINAS RIVER

SITE OF $5,000.00
LOUIS BELCHER
TREASURE, 1819
PADRE-INDIAN
ACTIVITIES AND
POSSIBLE SITE OF
LOST MISSION TREASURE

FABLED BANDIT LOOT
OF TIBURCIO VASQUEZ

LITTLE SUR
RIVER

PICO
BLANCO

CARMEL RIVER

CARMEL VALLEY ROAD

POINT
SUR

SOUTH FORK

BIG SUR

SILVER KING
MINE AND UNCLE AL'S
LOST WORLD

VENTANA DOUBLE CONE

BIG SUR RIVER

APPROXIMATE LOCATIONS OF THE JAKE
SCOTT MINE, THE FRANK PARIS TREASURE,
THE TRAMPA CANYON MINE AND THE
MYSTERY HOLE OF THE CACHAGUA-
CARMEL VALLEY ROAD.

RUMORED SITE OF
LOST MISSION MINE

LOST
VALLEY

PACIFIC OCEAN

WILLOW CREEK

RUMORED SITES OF THE
LOST VENTANA MINE AND
THE LOST PADRE MINE

DISAPPEARANCE
OF $50,000.00 IN
SPANISH GOLD COINS

The maps on these two pages are meant to help ori-
ent the reader with the various areas described and
discussed in this book. The maps are not meant to
serve as treasure guides and should not be considered as such. If one plans to search for the Monterey area's hidden riches, permission must be
gained from property owners as well
as proper authorities.

CAPE
SAN MARTIN

LOS BURROS
MINING DISTRICT
(over 2,000 claims registered)

6

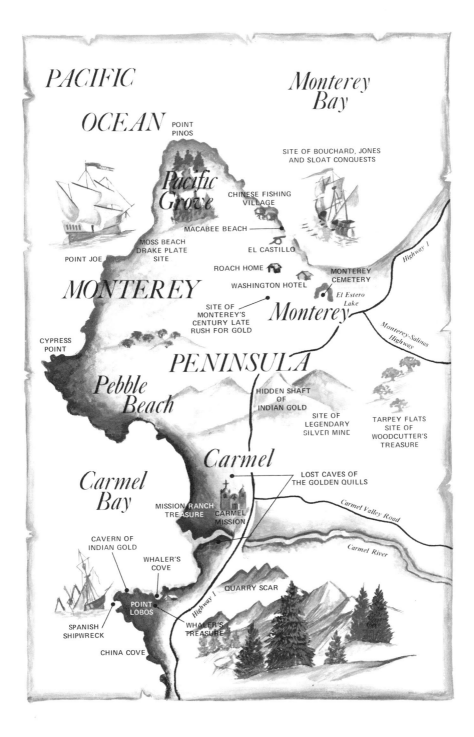

PACIFIC

OCEAN POINT PINOS

Monterey Bay

SITE OF BOUCHARD, JONES AND SLOAT CONQUESTS

Pacific Grove

CHINESE FISHING VILLAGE

MACABEE BEACH

MOSS BEACH DRAKE PLATE SITE

POINT JOE

EL CASTILLO

ROACH HOME

MONTEREY

WASHINGTON HOTEL

MONTEREY CEMETERY

El Estero Lake

SITE OF MONTEREY'S CENTURY LATE RUSH FOR GOLD

Monterey

CYPRESS POINT

Highway 1

Monterey-Salinas Highway

PENINSULA

Pebble Beach

HIDDEN SHAFT OF INDIAN GOLD

SITE OF LEGENDARY SILVER MINE

TARPEY FLATS SITE OF WOODCUTTER'S TREASURE

Carmel

Carmel Bay

LOST CAVES OF THE GOLDEN QUILLS

MISSION RANCH TREASURE

CARMEL MISSION

Carmel Valley Road

CAVERN OF INDIAN GOLD

WHALER'S COVE

Carmel River

QUARRY SCAR

POINT LOBOS

Highway 1

SPANISH SHIPWRECK

WHALER'S TREASURE

CHINA COVE

7

CONTENTS

TALES, TREASURES AND PIRATES OF OLD MONTEREY contains over thirty illustrations. Included in the illustrations are many rare and historically important photographs. With this collection of photographs to help document the tales, the book takes on added meaning and adds considerably to its historic value.

TALES OF
TREASURES
AND
LONG AGO HAPPENINGS

Although Indians have lived on the land surrounding Monterey Bay for thousands of years, and aged records tell of explorers trodding its paths as many as four centuries ago, the true history of the Monterey Peninsula has its beginning in the year 1770. It was on May 31st of this year – over two centuries ago – that Father Junipero Serra (the founder of Carmel Mission and California's famed Mission Trail) sailed into Monterey's rounded bay. On June 3rd of this year the City of Monterey was officially founded and, for all intents and purposes, this date also marks the beginning of tales of treasures that began to circulate around Alta California's remote "land of plenty".

With the local Costonoan Indians reportedly showing the padres handfuls of "yellow sand", and with stories of "gold for the taking" spreading throughout Monterey's meager Spanish outpost, it was not long before the Presidio soldiers took to the hills in search of Alta California's hidden wealth.

Many of the tales that excited these pioneer residents have been passed from generation to generation, and to this day many of these very same tales still stir the imagination and excite modern-day treasure seekers.

One of the most popular of the early Indian tales tells of a gold mine – known today as the Lost Ventana Mine. There are many stories concerning this lost bonanza but, in sifting the facts and comparing the notes, two legends stand out as the most probable – each bearing a striking resemblance to the other.

The first of these tales states the Lost Ventana Mine is but a day's walking distance from the Mission. The mine is said to be on a direct southeasterly course from a large white scar on the face of a nearby Santa Lucia peak. This peak, with its clearly visible cliff-side scar, is only a short distance from the mission and can easily be seen from the bell tower.

The scar referred to in this legend is the remains of a sandstone quarry where the Christianized Indians gathered stone used in the building of the church. History tells us these hard-working neophytes would chop a stone from their eagle-like perch, let it tumble down the the steep Lucia peak, and from the valley below carry it to the site of the present-day church.

Ventana, Spanish for "window", fits nicely into the tale as from the entrance to their nugget-filled cave one is said to be able to see the bell tower of the distant Carmel Mission.

As the story goes, the church fathers swore the Indians to secrecy, but, as so often happens with stories of gold, the secret was not long in leaking out. Treasure seekers have been searching for the "lost window" of the Lucias ever since.

Mission San Carlos de Borromeo del Rio Carmelo, known today as Carmel Mission, as it appeared on an early post card. It was from this church (the second in California's long line of missions) that Padre Junipero Serra's mission Indians are said to have headed south and obtained gold from a mine hidden deep in the Santa Lucias. Many early miners felt this lost bonanza was in the area of Monterey County's Los Burros Mining District. Credit — R.A. Reinstedt Collection.

The second tale of the Lost Ventana Mine states that the name of the mine was taken from a tall, almost inaccessible, peak approximately twenty-one air miles from the mission. This peak also lies in a southeasterly direction and is commonly referred to as Ventana Double Cone. As in the first story, Carmel Mission's bell tower plays a part in the tale, as legend states one is able to see the bell tower of the mission from the lofty summit of this peak.

It is of interest to note, in a southeasterly direction from the mission, Ventana Double Cone (at 4,833 feet) is one of the highest mountains of the Santa Lucia Range.

Continuing in a southerly direction from the summit of Double Cone peak, a day's walk brought the Indians to a cave where they obtained their yellow sand and golden pebbles.

Credibility of this story stems from the fact that gold has been, and still is, mined in a southerly direction from the Ventana peak. Continuing down the coastal range, approximately thirty-five air miles south of Ventana Double Cone (quite a day's hike over the rugged Santa Lucia Mountains), one will come upon the Los Burros Mining District.

Found in this southern tip of Monterey County are the remains of several long-forgotten gold mines. As a matter of record there were over 2,000 claims registered in the Los Burros district — 500 of them in an eight-square-mile area! Many of these claims never produced color, but a surprising number of them did. An estimate by the United States Bureau of Mines states the Last Chance Mine of the Los Burros Mining District (discovered on March 24, 1887) yielded $62,000.00 in valuable gold ore. With the Last Chance Mine being the best producer of ore, but being only one of several gold-producing mines, one can readily see that there was gold to be found in the Santa Lucias. With this in mind, one must admit there is the distinct possibility that Indians of long ago did find gold in the rugged mountains south of Carmel Mission. (For those interested in finding out more about Monterey's lost mother lode, a complete pictorial history of the Los Burros Mining District can be found in "Monterey's Mother Lode", by Randall A. Reinstedt. For further information see page two of this publication.)

With the above information lending authenticity to the story of the Lost Ventana Mine, as well as to such tales as the Lost Padre Mine (also said to be in the Los Burros area) and the Lost City of the

Santa Lucias (which in reality was the Los Burros mining community of Manchester), one begins to look at tales of hidden treasures and long-lost Indian riches in a new light.

Residents of the Los Burros Mining District's community of Manchester gather for a picture (thought to have been taken in the early 1890s). The mining community was destroyed by fire near the turn of the century, and is often referred to as the Lost City of the Santa Lucias. Credit — Monterey Savings & Loan Collection.

While discussing the mines of Monterey's south coast, an account of Big Sur's "Lost World" might be of interest. As we have learned from aged records of the Monterey area, the Spanish explorers of long ago tramped through the Big Sur wilderness (approximately twenty-five miles south of Carmel Mission), but apparently stopped only long enough to gaze at the scenery and bestow a name on its river — Rio Grande del Sur, meaning The Big River of the South.

Even though the Spanish didn't spend a great deal of time exploring the hundreds of canyons and peaks of the coastal range, accounts state they expressed more than just a passing interest in the tales of gold and silver that were said to be found in this land of rugged mountains and breathtaking vistas.

One such tale, involving both Spanish and Indians, tells how the Indians living near the Little Sur River (a spring-fed stream five miles north of the Big Sur River) would, upon the request of the Spanish, lead their burros into the Pico Blanco (White Mountain or Peak) area of the Little Sur and return the next day, their burros heavily laden with wire silver.

To the Spaniards' chagrin, the Indians "discouraged" company as they obediently headed for their mountain mine. It was not until many years later, when Alfred K. Clark began prospecting in the Little Sur area, that the legend of the lost silver mine was revived by the people of the Sur.

Clark, or Uncle Al as he was known to many, was a Union Army veteran who headed west after the Civil War and homesteaded on the South Fork of the Little Sur River. It was not long until he learned his land was in the area of a legendary silver mine.

Befriending one of the last surviving members of the Little Sur Indians (thought to have been of Esselen descent), Clark was eventually taken into his confidence, and years later, as the Indian lay near death, he revealed to Clark the details of the mine.

Discovering this lost bonanza to be within the shadows of towering Pico Blanco, Clark began a search that obsessed him to the day he died. It was not long before he found traces of silver in the area the Indian had described. Dreaming of untold riches, Clark immediately headed north — seeking financial backing.

Dr. Clarence H. Pearce (of the San Francisco area) listened intently to his story and soon became a full-fledged partner and financial backer. A tunnel was started at the spot Clark had found the silver, but after months of backbreaking labor, and nothing of commercial value to show for their efforts, Pearce became disenchanted and pulled out of the venture.

Clark was discouraged, but he vowed to dig on. Months passed when he would not be seen or heard from. Occasionally he would pack out of the hills and work as a ranch hand for Alvin Dani, foreman at the nearby Cooper Ranch.

Upon earning enough to stock his cupboards, Clark would pack his supplies on the back of a burro he had caught and tamed, and off they would go to a mountain cabin and a never-ending dream of lost riches.

Months turned into years and Uncle Al became a living legend of the Sur. He was often talked about, but seldom seen. Because he shied away from people and acted peculiarly, he was considered crazy by some and eccentric by others. People believed he had dreamed of silver too long, and was so obsessed by this dream he could not be rational about other things.

Stories circulated throughout the Sur that he had let his hair grow long to play the part of Uncle Sam in the 1915 San Francisco Exposition. Others say he was completely sane, but through misdealings and the chasing of poachers off his property, he had come to distrust all but a few close friends.

Of these friends, Al Geer and his family (one of the pioneer Sur families) became the most trusted. It was Al Geer who took Clark into his home when he was sick, and it was Geer who financed one of Uncle Al's last requests — a plane ride over his homestead and over the hidden entrance to the mine he had spent the greater part of his life working.

Clark was close to ninety when this took place; the year was 1930 and Uncle Al knew he was near death. The Geer family nursed him as best they could, but pneumonia finally took his life.

Before he died Clark gathered the Geer family around him and told them his land was theirs. It was then that he rambled on and told them the strangest tale they had ever heard.

Uncle Al admitted he never struck it rich in silver, but, in continuing, he told a story that, if authentic, could be worth far more to historians than a silver deposit ever would be.

One day while digging at the face of the wall in one of the underground shafts, Clark told of breaking into a mysterious hidden chamber. (Uncle Al's mine — the Silver King — led directly into the mountain approximately fifteen feet, then dropped twenty feet to the main shaft which, in turn, had separate tunnels branching off from it.)

Peering into the darkened room, he was dumfounded at the vastness of the cavern. Taking his light he crawled through the narrow opening and began to explore the underground chamber.

Slowly making his way from one subterranean room to another, Clark's light showed icicle-like formations stretching down from the ceilings and, at his feet, cone shaped outcroppings that rose from the floor.

In continuing with his story, Clark told of seeing strange stone

Alfred K. Clark's homestead "within the shadows of towering Pico Blanco" (seen in the background) was also the site of Big Sur's lost world of woolly mammoths and eyeless fish. The Little Sur River, as seen in the foreground, winds its way to the nearby Pacific. Credit — R.A. Reinstedt Collection.

Al Clark's completed cabin as it appeared in the early 1930s, after Clark's death. Early Big Sur Geer and Day families are shown in front of the cabin with their pack mules. Credit — Ruby Woicekowski Collection.

15

Alfred K. Clark (Uncle Al), legend of legends and discoverer of the Silver King Mine as well as Big Sur's mysterious subterranean world. Credit — Ruby Woicekowski Collection.

flowers that grew from the walls. Farther on, while passing into another chamber, his light fell upon a far wall where small shiny objects sparkled their reflections back to him. In one room Uncle Al recalled seeing a bubbling stream that contained peculiar looking white fish.

But most wondrous of all was an immense room which boasted a dry floor, pock-marked with well-worn Indian mortars, and strange paintings on the walls — depicting "elephants with long shaggy hair and curly teeth" and "cats with long sharp teeth".

As unbelievable as these discoveries seem, particularly when one considers they were described by a delirious old man who was considered eccentric by many, it is of interest to note there is a plausible scientific explanation for all that Clark described.

The great majority of the rock in the area of the Silver King is limestone. Pico Blanco itself is reported to contain the highest quality of dolomite limestone found on the central coast. Limestone is the type of rock that lends itself to such things as subterranean carvings by underground rivers.

The South Fork of the Little Sur River is said to disappear into the ground a short distance from where the mine is thought to be and reappears approximately one mile downstream. The albino fish Clark describes could be troglobites — blind fish that lose their body pigment due to the length of time they have lived in darkness.

The icicle type formations on the ceilings of the chambers could be stalactites, and the cone shaped objects on the floors could be stalagmites. These strange formations are often found in caves where there is a high content of lime, and they are formed from the evaporation of dripping mineralized water.

The stone flowers seen on the walls could be what geologists commonly refer to as gypsum flowers — so called because of the petal-like appearance produced when a substance called selenite extrudes from cave walls.

The shiny objects that reflected Clark's light could have been caused by a variety of different things, the most probable explanation being that the wall contained flakes of different minerals — silver perhaps included.

The prehistoric animal paintings probably depict the mammoth or mastodon and the saber-tooth tiger. These creatures are known to have roamed the California area before becoming extinct. There are other pictographs found on cave walls in close proximity to Clark's underground chambers, but none show any resemblance to creatures of the past.

The mortar holes on the cavern floor only add additional interest to an already unbelievable subterranean world – a world that perhaps at one time was inhabited by a forgotten culture.

When Uncle Al finished telling his tale, he told how he carefully sealed the chamber and spent the remainder of his days keeping strangers away from his lost world.

Not long after Clark died, the Geer family moved to his homestead. After a long search they found the entrance to the Silver King, but when they did, the tunnel was caved in. All attempts to reopen the mine proved futile.

With the passing of years numerous additional attempts have been made to clear the tunnel and to discover a natural entrance to the underground chambers. Many Indian artifacts have been found in the process, and there are ridges that are said to produce a strange hollow echo when horses gallop across, but to date there is no positive proof of Uncle Al's mammoth caves.

The homestead was eventually sold and the Geer family reluctantly moved on, but to this day believers in Uncle Al's hidden world search the slopes of Pico Blanco, hoping to find an entrance to the underground world of Alfred K. Clark. Perhaps, through the perseverance of these south coast searchers, stories will once again circulate throughout the Sur of a mysterious subterranean world. . . a world boasting woolly mammoths and eyeless fish!

In moving up the coast from the area of the Little Sur River, one comes upon the rocky shore line of the Point Lobos State Reserve. Internationally known as "The greatest meeting of land and water in the world", this jagged and beautiful "Point of the Sea Wolves" boasts more than its share of long-lost treasures. One tale, which includes Indians and gold, tells of a mysterious cave near the tip of the point which was accessible only at special times during the year. The entrance to this cave was below the water line, and an extreme minus tide was required before one could gain entrance.

The cliff above the cave was a sheer drop, and the water in the narrow cove in which the cave was located was choppy and rough. For these reasons the Indians ingeniously lowered themselves down the face of the cliff with a rope of fibers they had patiently woven.

Inside the cave the constant churning of the Pacific waters had washed bits of gold from the cavern's walls. All that was left for the Indians to do was scoop up the nuggets and flakes that lay on the floor.

Unfortunately, the entrance to this cavern collapsed in the 1940s, and from all indications mother nature did a remarkable job of sealing the entrance to this underwater grotto.

In discussing the possibilities of gold in this Costonoan cavern with an elderly Montereyan who had ventured into the cave as a boy, he only laughed and commented, "The only color that I found in the cave was the red and black abalone that clung to its ceiling and walls."

Point Lobos is famous for its scenic vistas. The precipice shown in the above illustration is a part of the Point Lobos Reserve and indicates the ruggedness of its picturesque shoreline. Perhaps it was this point that contained the hidden Costonoan cavern and claimed the Spanish ship carrying a fortune in gold. Credit — R.A. Reinstedt Collection.

P robably the most popular Point Lobos treasure tale tells of a Spanish ship boasting a large quantity of gold that was long ago wrecked on its rocky point. Legend states there were three survivors who miraculously made their way to shore – each burdened with a portion of the ship's valuable cargo.

After carefully sighting through the crotch of an old cypress tree, these fortunate seafarers buried the ship's gold where a gnarled limb pointed.

Making their way into Monterey, the grateful survivors celebrated their good fortune at a local saloon. It was not long before the free-flowing whiskey loosened the tongue of one of the boastful three. Before his companions realized what was taking place, he told the story of the buried treasure.

In the brawl that followed two of the sailors were killed and the third mysteriously disappeared.

An Indian working as a whaler at the nearby Portuguese-operated Whaler's Cove (today a part of the Point Lobos Reserve) once told of finding the gold after locating the gnarled limb that pointed to its hiding place. He described in detail how he dug in the dead of night, and just as his shovel hit the treasure a strange and eerie glow appeared through the cypress trees.

The superstitious Indian, thinking the devil had most assuredly caught him, frantically filled in the hole and vowed never to return. . ., or tell where the treasure was buried.

O ther events taking place in the Point Lobos area long before the turn of the century included such profitable pastimes as the smuggling of Chinese. In 1882, with the introduction of the Chinese Exclusion Bill, this unlawful business came into its own.

China Cove, located on the southerly side of Point Lobos, is said to have gained its name from this thriving business.

One pioneer ship captain is rumored to have favored this secluded cove over any on the coast. As his disciplined crew laboriously unloaded their human cargo, he would place his first mate in command and mysteriously slip away in his small dinghy.

Loaded aboard this minature boat would be a chest filled with valuables. Legend states this "Captain's Treasure" is still hidden in one of the many natural caves found near China Cove.

China Cove, a part of the Point Lobos Reserve, boasts a history of smuggling. It is also said to be the site of a "Captain's treasure", buried in one of the many natural caves in the area (two of which can be seen in the photograph). Credit — R.A. Reinstedt Collection.

The most recent known treasure hunt in the Point Lobos area took place in 1932. In that year three treasure seekers came to the Monterey Peninsula from its northerly neighbor of San Francisco.

They set up camp on the grounds of Carmel Mission, and with the help of a "custom made" divining rod they made many interesting discoveries near the church.

One evening, while exploring the nearby hills of Point Lobos, their detector recorded a strong indication of buried metal. The location was in a small swale behind an old whaler's cabin (this cabin still stands near the south-west shore of Whaler's Cove).

With darkness creeping in, accompanied by a covering of damp

Monterey fog, a decision to dig for the metal with the first rays of morning light was agreed upon by all. Early the following morning, as the treasure seekers eagerly approached the swale, they were shocked to discover a freshly dug hole with the rusted imprint of a large metal chest at the bottom.

What was in the chest, or who dug it up, has never been determined, but there is general agreement that it was originally the property of a Portuguese whaler who, as was the custom of the day, had buried his savings for safekeeping.

The swale behind this aged whaler's cabin (built in 1868) in the Point Lobos Reserve is where a freshly-dug hole was found — leaving the rusted imprint of a large metal chest. Credit — R.A. Reinstedt Collection.

Whaler's Cove, also a part of Point Lobos Reserve, whose colorful history of whaling dates back to 1855. Many early tales tell of Portuguese whalers who, long before the turn of the century, buried their savings around Whaler's Cove, preferring to trust the bank of mother nature rather than their fellow men. By the time this picture was taken in the early 1900s the whaling industry had been replaced by the hunting and canning of abalones. Credit – Allen Knight Maritime Museum Collection.

C armel Mission, within sight of picturesque Point Lobos, and as illustrated in the tales of the Lost Ventana Mine, includes numerous tales of treasure in its proud heritage. As a matter of record, many of the Monterey area's most remarkable treasure tales are connected with the history of this beautiful church.

One tale, which includes long-ago happenings at Point Lobos, as well as events related to Monterey's encounter with the bold Pacific pirate Hippolyte Bouchard (discussed elsewhere in this publication), will serve as an introduction to a selected number of treasure tales linked to Carmel's famed church.

In the year of 1818 Bouchard attacked and burned the town of Monterey, gained control of the Presidio, and spread considerable panic over the entire area.

The word of this pirate and his army of evil men soon reached the fathers at Carmel Mission. The quick thinking padres, not wanting to risk the church valuables, loaded many of the prized possessions onto the back of a blind Indian and led him into the hills where the treasures were carefully buried.

Taking care to hide the ornaments where no one would chance upon them, the padres returned to the mission after dark, secure in their belief that neither pirates, nor anyone else, would carry away their cherished possessions. With Bouchard making a nuisance of himself for the better part of a week, the padres were not able to return for their valuables for several days. When the time finally came to retrieve their treasures, the padres were unable to find them. Legend states several golden altar ornaments, jeweled chalices, and ornate candelabra are, to this day, buried in the foothills of the Santa Lucias.

Of course, if one is a Robert Louis Stevenson enthusiast, he may believe this very same church treasure was hidden in a blow hole in the Point Lobos area. In 1879, when Stevenson lived in Monterey, he, in the company of a trusted friend, searched many a Point Lobos crevice for this legendary treasure.

Perhaps a final note should be added to this tale as, according to church authorities, nothing was taken from the church during the Bouchard reign of terror. To this day they proudly claim that Carmel Mission has in its inventory the very same objects that it had when Bouchard made his appearance over a century and a half ago.

I n continuing with mission-oriented treasure tales, the following two stories should help to illustrate the enormous number of legends the mission Indians passed on to the old-timers of the Monterey area.

These two tales concern "The Lost Caves of the Golden Quills". Both of the caves are said to have been near Carmel Mission, and both contained ledges that had been laboriously carved into their rock walls. In days of long ago the ledges contained an assortment of bird feathers, generally agreed to have been from the ever-present seagull. Inside the hollow quills of these feathers the Indians poured small flakes of gold and large quantities of gold dust.

Why gold was poured into the hollows of bird feathers is open to question. Some suggest this was just a novel way of storing the gold, while others claim it was done in an attempt to fool their enemies. Perhaps the Indians reasoned. . . , who would guess to look into the hollow of a bird feather for a valuable treasure? (Additional research has shown other California Indian tribes, as well as miners from New Mexico, were also in the habit of using the hollows of bird feathers in which to store gold.)

Although both caves were located close to the mission, they are reported to have been in different directions. One is said to have been at the base of a gentle rolling hill near a lagoon at the mouth of the Carmel River, this particular hill being marked today by a wooden cross at its summit. The second cave was but a few hundred yards from the mission, located deep in a ravine to the north of the church and halfway up a steep, rocky cliff.

Needless to say, "The Lost Caves of the Golden Quills" have long since been stripped of their wealth, and rain, wind and time have long since concealed their entrances to all but the gods.

With many of the mission treasure tales ending on a somewhat negative note, one story of a treasure that was found will, perhaps, help to rekindle the spark of future treasure seekers.

In the vicinity of Carmel's aged church are the grounds of the historic Mission Ranch (many of the original ranch buildings are in use to this day, and are frequented by numerous Peninsula residents and visitors). Over the years portions of the ranch land were cultivated and a surprising number of crops were grown. During this period of time the Mission Ranch foreman was a busy man and was constantly on the lookout for extra help.

It is one of the hired hands that this tale is about. Early one afternoon the man in question brought in the plow animals and complained of not feeling well. Being a hard worker and a trusted helper, the foreman sympathized with the man and told him to "Put up the horses and take the rest of the afternoon off."

When the hired hand failed to report for work the following morning the foreman dutifully harnessed the horses and proceeded with plans to complete the plowing. Upon reaching the spot where the plow had been left, the foreman was suddenly made very much aware of why his hired hand had not returned to work. Not more than a few feet from the blade of the plow was a neatly dug hole — its outline revealing the imprint of a large iron pot.

The pot, along with its contents, was not to be found, and with its having been common knowledge among old-timers that a pot of gold coins had once been buried on the ranch, it didn't take the foreman long to realize that his trusted helper's ill health was probably the result of a somewhat common early California ailment. . . , sometimes referred to as "gold fever".

Tales of iron pots harboring hoards of riches are certainly not new to the Monterey Peninsula. A second iron pot — leaving a telltale imprint as proof it was there — was taken from the Monterey area approximately one century ago.

To appreciate this tale, one must be aware of the circumstances surrounding it. In the autumn of 1877, California's most noted villain, Joaquin Murieta, was reported to have been in the area of the Los Laureles Ranch (approximately halfway between the communities of Monterey and Salinas). What makes this rather hard to believe is the fact that 1877 was nearly a quarter of a century after Murieta was supposedly killed (with his head being decapitated as proof) by Captain Harry S. Love and the California Rangers. In an effort to add credence to the Monterey tale of treasure, it must be noted that many historians claim it was Joaquin Valenzuela (a second known California bandit) whom Captain Love's Rangers killed in the much publicized 1853 encounter. These very same historians state that Joaquin Murieta and his lovely wife Rosita spent the remaining years of their lives with their people in northern Mexico.

With the above information as background, Monterey's second tale of an iron pot treasure takes on added meaning. According to an early documented account, Joaquin Murieta was seen, befriended, and spent at least one night in the Los Laureles area. Not only was he seen, but upon questioning he admitted to two old-timers that he was the once-feared Mother Lode bandit, and that he had only returned to claim a pot of treasure left by his gang twenty plus years before.

The following morning Murieta was gone, and at the base of a large oak tree near the present-day intersection of the Los Laureles grade and the Salinas-Monterey highway, a freshly dug hole was discovered — with the telltale imprint of a rusted iron caldron at its bottom.

California's notorious Joaquin Murieta, as portrayed by an early artist. Of course, in 1877, when Joaquin returned to the Monterey area to retrieve his bandit booty, he did not appear as young and dashing as he did in the above rendering. Credit — California State Library Collection.

hile on the subject of California bad men, as well as aged treasures in the outlying areas of old Monterey, a tale or two of Tiburcio Vasquez — Monterey's infamous bandit — should be included. Second only to Joaquin Murieta as California's most noted villain, Vasquez was born in the capital city of Monterey in 1835.

With Vasquez's life an open book, there are several accounts to choose from in describing his "dastardly deeds" in and around the Monterey area. Perhaps the one that portrays him best tells how he would take great pleasure in hiding away at the home of his sister who lived directly behind the Monterey jail. After daring escapades into the heart of Monterey, Vasquez would slip back to his sister's adobe and watch the harassed sheriff organize a posse and ride off in search of the "home-grown" desperado.

On one such episode the sheriff was tipped off and, as his men surrounded the house, Tiburcio beat a hasty retreat — barely escaping with his life and his loot.

As far as a local Vasquez treasure is concerned, a goodly amount of bandit booty is said to await some lucky finder on a ranch in upper Carmel Valley. The name of the ranch is Palo Escrito which, roughly translated, means written tree. The name, legend states, was gained from a huge old oak tree boasting a coded message carved into its gnarled trunk. Carved by Tiburcio Vasquez himself, this elaborately engraved message is said to have been the key to a vast fortune he buried near the aged, and since fallen, tree.

From the parlor of this adobe, situated directly across the street from the jail, Monterey-born villain Tiburcio Vasquez often watched the sheriff organize posses and ride off in search of the elusive bandit. Credit — R.A. Reinstedt Collection.

While waiting to be hung in the San Jose jail, noted bad man Tiburcio Vasquez posed for pictures (above) and was described as the epitome of an elegant Mexican Don. Credit — Robert Couchman Collection.

*A*dditional treasures waiting to be found in the upper reaches of the sun-drenched Carmel Valley include the relatively unknown riches of long-ago resident Frank Paris. With visions of visiting his homeland of France, Paris hoarded his savings for many years. With surprising regularity he added to his treasure of five, ten and twenty-dollar gold pieces. Hiding his money in a can, Paris buried his hard-earned wages in a dry creek bed near his cabin (near the mouth of Carmel Valley's Cachagua country). After one particularly heavy winter rain, Paris hurried out to check his savings — only to discover that the once dry creek bed was now a raging mountain stream. Through the briskly flowing water Paris saw that his can had been washed from its hiding place and carried away by the swiftly flowing river. . . , never to be seen again.

*A*lso in Carmel Valley's Cachagua country are the remains of a once profitable mine. Even though copper was the main mineral of importance, considerable amounts of gold and silver are also listed as having been found. The mine, located in the remote Trampa Canyon area of the Cachagua, was actively worked in the late 1800s and finally succumbed to water in the shaft. Efforts of the day to drain and pump the deep shaft proved fruitless, but with new techniques and modern technology, who knows what Carmel Valley's Trampa Canyon mine would yield today?

A second attempt at mining in Carmel Valley takes us back to the 1860s. In that long-ago year Jake Scott, said to have been a miner from California's famed Mother Lode, drifted to the Monterey-Salinas area. With thoughts of gold uppermost in his mind, he scoured the nearby countryside searching for a likely spot in which to "strike it rich". Finally, homesteading in the area now known as Hastings Reservation, he built a cabin and a barn (which still stands), and then turned to his first love — prospecting. Laboriously digging tunnels and shafts in the lava-type rock of Red Mountain, Jake Scott spent many fruitless years searching for the elusive yellow ore. Today, one crumbling shaft is all that remains of his dream of a Carmel Valley mother lode.

This "dynamite-hewn" barn was built in 1863 by Carmel Valley prospector Jake Scott. Credit — R.A. Reinstedt Collection.

Over a century ago Jake Scott spent many years in upper Carmel Valley searching for gold. The above photo shows all that is left of three large tunnels that he painstakingly dug into the lava-type rock of Red Mountain. Unfortunately, no gold was found, and Jake Scott's dream of a Carmel Valley mother lode was never realized. Credit — R.A. Reinstedt Collection.

As described in the story below, the above illustration shows the crumbling ruins of the Robinson Canyon cabin where Robert Louis Stevenson was nursed back to health in the long-ago year of 1879. Credit — R.A. Reinstedt Collection.

Closer to the Monterey Peninsula, but still a part of Carmel Valley, is a beautiful country canyon boasting a most colorful history. Robinson Canyon, as it is known, is perhaps most noted for harboring the decayed remains of an aged cabin where the world-famed author Robert Louis Stevenson was nursed back to health after being saved from almost certain death. Other interesting aspects of the history of this picturesque valley canyon include the stories of numerous mysterious visits by padres and Indians in the long-ago year of 1819. With tales of baptisms and marriages taking place in the canyon, combined with stories of old-timers finding an ancient oak tree with a cross and the initials I.H.S. carved into its trunk (as well as a grave with a weathered wooden cross), one begins to wonder just what the activities were that took place in this remote valley wilderness. Some think the visits were a result of Bouchard's nightmarish attack on Monterey in 1818. Others think a futile search was being undertaken for Carmel Mission's lost church treasures. Still others speculate as to the possibility of a church outpost or rancho being constructed, possibly in anticipation of future attacks by Pacific privateers. These are good guesses, and perhaps one of them is accurate. Unfortunately for local historians, the hope of finding out what actually did take place in Carmel Valley's Robinson Canyon over a century and a half ago becomes a little less promising with each passing year.

With Robinson Canyon's activities of 1819 remaining an unsolved mystery, perhaps a tale of treasure will serve as a change of pace and bring us back to the subject at hand. Aside from historic cabins and strange goings-on, this Carmel Valley canyon is rumored to be the site of a $5,000.00 cache of gold coins. (Before one jumps to conclusions, it should be mentioned that this treasure was buried long after 1819!) With lost gold coins to whet the appetite, it becomes of even more interest to serious seekers of fortunes when they learn that Louis Belcher, a principal player in the famed Sanchez treasure feud, was the man who stashed this unfound money!

With the mention of the Sanchez treasure, it would be truly unjust to continue with tales of the Monterey area's hidden wealth without an account of the circumstances surrounding this lost bonanza.

Don Jose Maria Sanchez was a wealthy Spanish Californian who owned a large and prosperous ranch near the busy mission town of San Juan Bautista. He was known throughout the Monterey Bay area and was admired by all who knew him.

One blustery December evening, while returning from a cattle drive to California's famed gold country, Don Jose approached the last obstacle between him and his San Juan hacienda. Stopping at the rain-swollen Pajaro River, Sanchez thought of spending the night, but thoughts of his wife and family only a few miles beyond were too much for him to resist. Urging his mount into the swift-flowing water, Sanchez was swept from his horse and never seen again.

Talk of Don Jose's death quickly spread throughout the Monterey Bay communities. Speculation arose over what would become of his family, his wealth, and his 40,000-acre ranch. In the 1850s a widow was looked upon as "legitimate prey" by California's collection of misfits and outlaws. The land was still ruled by the six-shooter, and the bullet reigned as final judge.

At this point in history, the law of Monterey County lay in the capable hands of Sheriff William Roach. Roach was a mountain of a man who kept law and order with his fists as well as his guns.

It was not long after the death of Don Jose that Roach offered his services to the heartbroken Sanchez widow. A bargain was soon struck, with William Roach giving up his job as sheriff and becoming administrator of the wealthy Sanchez estate.

Monterey as it appeared about the time of the Sanchez treasure feud (early 1850s). The drawing is a woodcut reproduction of a John Russell Bartlett picture. Credit — Monterey Savings & Loan Collection.

As Roach saw it, one of his first duties was to remove a portion of the Sanchez treasure from the hacienda and hide it in a safe place. Taking seventeen sacks of gold dust (each containing $5,000.00) from a huge barrel where it had been carelessly thrown, Roach transported the treasure to his Monterey home. In the dead of night Roach and his wife placed the gold in a steel box, carefully pried up a portion of the floor, hid the gold in the adobe foundation, replaced the floor boards, and placed a camphorwood chest over the floor above it.

For two years the $85,000.00 Sanchez treasure remained hidden in the foundation of the Roach home. While the gold was secured in its Monterey hide-a-way, several events took place which divided the community of Monterey into two factions, creating considerable ill will among many of its citizens.

The first eighteen months of the two-year tenure were without incident, with Roach doing a remarkable job as administrator of the estate. Not only was he successful in keeping the outlaws and misfits away from the land, but he also succeeded in building up the large herds of cattle, sheep and horses.

A year and a half after the untimely death of Sanchez, his widow married a Yankee doctor by the name of Walter Sanford. It was Sanford's visit to Roach, with the information that he was no longer needed as administrator, and the request for the $85,000.00, that started a chain of events that were to rock the Monterey area for more than a decade.

Readily giving up his job as administrator, Roach balked at returning the gold without first pocketing the substantial sum of $35,000.00, which he calculated his 18-month tenure had been worth. Shocked at Roach's demand for such an exorbitant fee, Sanford vowed to take Roach to court and let a judge decide what was legal and just.

Unable to get a Monterey attorney to touch the case, Sanford hired David S. Terry, a well-known Stockton lawyer. A veteran of the Mexican war and the Texas struggle for independence, Terry was also a noted gun fighter, an expert with the bowie knife, and a talented lawyer. He loved a fight, whether it be in an alley or in a courtroom, and readily accepted the case.

After a fruitless visit to Roach, Terry devised a plan as cunning as it was lawless. Realizing it would be useless to bring the popular Roach to trial in his own home town, Terry proceeded to have him kidnapped on the premise of bringing him to trial in San Joaquin County where he was the accepted political boss.

Terry sent four hoodlums to Monterey armed with a warrant for the arrest of one William Roach, charging him with "defrauding the estate of Jose Maria Sanchez while acting as administrator."

These men succeeded in capturing Roach and hustling him out of Monterey under the cover of darkness. They rode only at night, following seldom used trails and out-of-the-way canyons.

Thrown into a kennel-like cell upon his arrival in Stockton, Roach was treated like an animal and placed under a twenty-four hour guard. Visited by Terry, Roach was informed he would go free, plus receive the sum of $20,000.00, if he were to hand over the remainder of the $85,000.00. Terry's offer only infuriated Roach and made him all the more defiant.

Feeling he would be rescued when, and if, his whereabouts became known, Roach refused to give in to Terry, and suffered through six agonizing months in his Stockton cell. As the months dragged by, Roach realized his strength, as well as his chances of rescue, were slipping away with each passing day and finally decided to accept Terry's offer.

Upon Roach's request, Frank Foote, his twenty-four hour guard, summoned Terry. It was Terry's and Sanford's visit to the Roach cell that proved to be the boomerang that turned Foote against his boss. After confronting their weakened prisoner, Roach agreed to write a note to his wife telling her to give up the gold, providing he would be set free and would be guaranteed the $20,000.00. Upon completion of the note, Terry grabbed it from Roach's feeble hand and laughed in his face, "You'll never see your $20,000.00, Roach. I'll watch you rot before you ever see a penny of that money!" With that remark Terry and Sanford stalked out of the building and began preparations for the long ride to Monterey.

Foote, who had learned to respect Roach during his six-month captivity, found it hard to believe the scene he had witnessed. He knew Terry to be a hard man, but he had always respected him as an honest man.

With Terry gone, Roach knew he had only one faint hope left. He told Foote the entire story. He also offered Foote the $85,000.00 treasure if he could beat Terry and Sanford to Monterey and get the gold before they could.

Accepting the challenge, Foote told Roach they would split the treasure if he succeeded in reaching Monterey first. Shooting the lock off the cell door, Foote got a second note to Roach's wife and set out on the fastest horse he could find.

Roach, being too weak to accompany Foote on his race to Monterey, remained in Stockton until he regained his strength.

Riding day and night Foote was successful in beating Terry and Sanford to Monterey. Upon reaching Roach's Monterey home, Foote's historic ride soon became the talk of the territory. He had ridden more than 150 miles in the unbelievable time of twenty-three hours! Being totally exhausted when he handed the note to Annie Roach, Foote was immediately taken to a nearby adobe where he was carefully hidden and placed under the watchful eye of a neighboring family.

Upon learning her husband was still alive, and realizing she was about to be visited by the two men who were responsible for his mysterious disappearance, the quick-thinking Annie Roach wisely summoned her brother, Jerry McMahon, who hurriedly pried up the floor boards of the Roach house and took the treasure from its hiding place.

With the treasure gone and nothing to hide, Terry and Sanford were greeted by a hostile and defiant Annie Roach. Infuriated by the sudden turn of events, Terry and Sanford tore the Roach house apart searching for the treasure. Finding nothing that resembled $85,000.00 in gold, the enraged duo went separate ways in an attempt to cool their tempers and relieve their frustrations.

Finding his way to the barroom of Monterey's Washington Hotel, Sanford met McMahon who had just returned from hiding the gold. An exchange of shots soon echoed throughout the barroom. . . , resulting in the death of both Sanford and McMahon! With the death of McMahon, so died the secret of the whereabouts of the $85,000.00 treasure! Jerry McMahon had not told a soul where he had buried the ill-fated fortune.

As the word of the shootings filtered throughout the town the citizens of Monterey began taking sides – the majority backed Roach, whom they warmly welcomed home, while others sided with Terry, believing Roach had had no right to hold the $85,000.00.

Upon learning of the killings, Don Jose's widow sobbed uncontrollably, repeatedly stating the gold was "truly cursed."

As tension mounted among the Montereyans, two of Roach's close friends, Isaac Wall and Tom Williamson, were cruelly murdered as they led a heavily-packed mule away from Monterey. It was surmised the murderer thought the mule carried the Sanchez fortune, but he was sadly mistaken when the packs were ripped open and only arms and camping supplies were found within.

The blame for this foul deed fell on the well-known bandit Anastasio Garcia, who had fallen in with Terry and his gang. Garcia, who is given the credit of training the previously mentioned Tiburcio Vasquez, was tracked to his cabin by Monterey's Sheriff Keating and a posse of his best men.

When the dust settled, three of Keating's men lay dead, and Garcia was still on the loose. He was subsequently captured in the Sierra Madre Mountains near Los Angeles and brought back to stand trial. . . , only to be hung in his jail cell while the population of Monterey attended church services.

This grave marker serving as a grim reminder of the Sanchez treasure feud, reads; "Ths. Williamson, murdered in Monterey County, 9 Nov. 1855". The marker is in Monterey's old Catholic Cemetery. It was Thomas Williamson and Isaac Wall, two of Roach's close friends, who were murdered as they led a heavily-packed mule away from Monterey. Credit — R.A. Reinstedt Collection.

In 1856 Louis Belcher, the young Monterey attorney who had originally suggested Sanford hire Terry (and the man responsible for the $5,000.00 Robinson Canyon treasure), was standing at the bar in the Washington Hotel talking with a close friend and member of the Terry gang. Suddenly a shot rang out from the street and Belcher fell to the floor. Harry Atwood, Belcher's partner at the bar, immediately ran out looking for the assailant. Unable to find a trace of who had done the killing, Atwood returned to the hotel late that night, placed a pistol to his head and committed suicide.

It is Louis Belcher's $5,000.00 in gold coins that is said to be buried in Carmel Valley's Robinson Canyon. It was also Louis Belcher who played a prominent role in, and became a casualty of, Monterey's Sanchez treasure feud. Credit — William A. Martin Collection.

Finally, William Roach met his end in November of 1866. He was ambushed near Watsonville and his battered body was found at the bottom of a well.

The brutal slaying of Roach ended the bloody trail of the "cursed" Sanchez treasure. Foote died four years later of smallpox, while trying to track down the murderers of his good friend Bill Roach.

Terry, who later became famous for his San Francisco shenanigans, eventually met death while Judge of the Supreme Court. He was shot by a United States Marshal after attacking a fellow judge in Lathrop, California.

This ends the tragic tale of Monterey's Sanchez treasure. Only the reader can judge whether the treasure was truly cursed. What we do know is that the gold has never been accounted for, and is said to still be buried in or around Monterey. For those who are interested there are also those who say. . . , the curse was only good for the first hundred years!

Opened in 1849, Monterey's Washington Hotel was, for many years, the area's most popular hostelry. During the days of the Sanchez treasure feud, the Washington Hotel was the scene of considerable bloodshed as Dr. Walter Sanford, Jerry McMahon, Louis Belcher and Harry Atwood all met violent deaths in the barroom of the hotel. Credit — Monterey Savings & Loan Collection.

*A*lso in the eventful 1850s, the robbery of an army pay wagon near the Presidio of Monterey caused considerable excitement and the loss of one life – the robber's.

As with the Sanchez fortune, the only person knowing the whereabouts of the treasure was shot and killed without divulging his secret.

Unlike the Sanchez fortune, the old-timers of Monterey seem to agree as to the whereabouts of this lost treasure.

In making his getaway the lone gunman was chased from the site of the robbery to the Monterey cemetery. Those familiar with the Monterey cemetery know that it is partially surrounded by a crescent shaped lake, which made the entrance and exit almost one way. Witnesses claimed to have seen the bandit enter the cemetery with the money. Some time later, upon attempting to escape the confines of the graveyard, the robber was shot and killed. A search of the body revealed no money.

There is general confusion as to how long the bandit was in the cemetery. Some say he was there such a short time it wouldn't have been possible for him to have buried his ill-fated fortune. They therefore agree he must have dropped it in a hollow of one of the many oak trees. Others say he hid out in the cemetery for quite a lengthy spell, affording him ample opportunity to bury his loot.

What actually became of the army payroll is still a mystery; there are no records of it ever having been found, and many old-timers feel it is still "planted" somewhere in the confines of the Monterey cemetery.

*T*he Monterey cemetery is said to also hold the remains of an undisclosed church treasure. As the story goes, many years ago a cemetery caretaker discovered strange markings on the trunk of an ancient oak tree. The most prominent of the aged carvings portrayed a large cross with an arrow at its base. Being an avid treasure hunter, and knowing that a symbol of this type indicated a church treasure was buried nearby, the caretaker wasted little time in bringing his metal detector to the site. Obtaining a reading near the base of the tree, the caretaker was granted permission for an exploratory dig, and excitedly set to work. At a two-foot depth he came upon a layer of old handmade

To this day, on a gnarled oak tree in the Monterey cemetery, the above cross —
boasting an arrowhead at its base — points to what many believe is an aged church
treasure. Credit — R.A. Reinstedt Collection.

bricks — not of the adobe variety. Using a crowbar he laboriously worked his way through the bricks.

With his metal detector now recording a much stronger reading, he continued his digging until he struck hardpan (extremely hard clay-like soil). Needing a jackhammer to continue the dig, permission was emphatically denied and the hole was ordered closed.

Whatever was there is there to this day, but there is considerable doubt as to whether permission will ever again be granted to "prospect" in the grounds of the Monterey cemetery.

N ot far from the Monterey cemetery is the site of the old Monterey airport. In the early days of Jennys and Wacos this area was known as Tarpey Flats — so named because Michael "Matt" Tarpey lost his life there on March 17, 1873 (Tarpey was hung from an oak tree by a vigilance committee which had taken him from the Monterey jail). Other than this most unfortunate lynching over a century ago, this area is also known for a treasure that was found there approximately fifty years later. It was on Tarpey Flats that a small band of woodcutters discovered what many believe was a sizeable fortune, quite possibly the loot of a long-forgotten robbery, or perhaps even more likely, the life savings of an early Montereyan.

Leaving for work one summer day, this band of woodsmen mysteriously vanished — never to be seen or heard from again. Upon following their trail into the oak-studded hills, all that was found was a cluster of footprints and a collection of abandoned tools.

A thorough search of the area revealed one other significant find. Deep in the hollow of a freshly cut tree were the traces of a long-forgotten cache of coins — showing signs of having been there for many years.

With this discovery the mystery of why the woodcutters suddenly left town was solved. But to this day the questions of to whom the treasure belonged, and how long it had been concealed in the gnarled old oak, remain a mystery.

W ithout a doubt, the most valuable treasure, at least according to local legends, to have been lost in the Monterey Bay area was the contents of a safe belonging to Tom Sing of Pacific Grove's picturesque Chinese fishing village. Said to have been a cook at a long-forgotten Monterey restaurant, Sing also is said to have owned the only safe in the Chinese community. For a fee, Sing stored gold and other valuables in his safe for residents of the unique waterfront village.

Taking place in the hectic years following California's rush for gold, Sing soon became Chinatown's "official" banker, and his safe was rumored to contain large quantities of Mother Lode gold. All went well until the mid 1870s, when three well-known San Francisco bank robbers heard of the "easy pickins" in Pacific Grove's Chinatown.

Making their way to the Monterey Peninsula, the San Franciscans succeeded in stealing the safe and making good their initial escape. Unfortunately for the bandits, they were unable to open their cumbersome cargo, and with it slowing their escape pace, they decided to bury the safe along the banks of the Salinas River (rumored to have been between Chualar and Gonzales). With a posse hot on their trail, it was not long after the safe was buried (and all telltale signs carefully removed) that the troubled trio were overtaken. Refusing to tell where the safe was buried, and found to be riding stolen mounts — San Francisco's safe robbers turned horse thieves met a quick end as they were promptly hung from a nearby tree. To this day the safe has never been found, and its contents are reported to have contained gold and valuables worth an estimated $780,000.00!

O ther not-so-well-known stories of Chinatown treasures are equally as intriguing as the long-lost safe of old Tom Sing. When Monterey had its own small version of a Chinatown, long after Pacific Grove's Chinese fishing village burned to the ground, stories circulated throughout Peninsula communities of vast sums of money that periodically changed hands on the gambling tables of old Monterey.

Among those involved in these long-ago games of chance were two Chinese gentlemen known as "Slim" and "Big Tom". With games between these two men sometimes lasting the better part of a week, and with hundreds of thousands of dollars amassed on the table tops, spectators from miles around were known to drop by and view the proceedings.

Of interest in this story is the tale of what "Big Tom" did with his winnings on the occasions he proved the victor. What money he did not send to far-off China is rumored to have been buried behind a restaurant and under the rocks of Monterey's Macabee Beach.

Main street of Monterey Bay's picturesque Chinese fishing village. It was from here that Tom Sing's heavily-laden safe was stolen by San Francisco bank robbers. Located near the area now known as Cannery Row, the village was only a "stone's-throw" from Macabee Beach and the site of Big Tom's treasure. Unfortunately for historians, and of course all who were involved, the Chinese fishing village burned to the ground (under questionable circumstances) in the long-ago year of 1906. Credit — Monterey History & Art Association Collection.

I n bringing to a close the numerous stories of Monterey's lost treasures, a final account — boasting an exciting tale of a treasure that was found — should help to end this narrative on a positive note.

Exactly one hundred years — to the month — after James Wilson Marshall discovered gold along California's American River, Monterey experienced its second rush for gold!

The news of this century-late gold strike broke with the publication of the January 12, 1948, issue of the Monterey Peninsula Herald. A front page article boasted a headline reading, "Gold Hoard Discovered In Monterey". (In actuality the word had leaked out to a limited few two days earlier and by the time the report appeared in the newspaper, over 125 twenty-dollar gold pieces had been found!)

As would be expected, within minutes after the newspaper was placed on the newsstands, the people of Monterey began heading for "gold hill".

In tracing the origin of this lost bonanza, it was found that the man responsible for the hidden hoard was a pioneer Montereyan by the name of Will Martin. Before his death in 1913, this respected citizen told his nephew, Carmel Martin (a past mayor of Monterey), that "money was buried on the place". Unfortunately he was unable to

Not allowed to dig until the working day was over for the construction crew, Monterey's 1948 seekers of fortunes patiently await the 5:00 p.m. "All Clear" signal (note one young lad whose patience got the best of him). Credit — W.L. Morgan Collection — Monterey Public Library.

pinpoint the exact location or tell the amount of how much he had buried.

By early evening the site of the Will Martin estate was swarming with people. Members of the Martin family were even reported to be on hand, with Carmel Martin himself cheerfully handing out an assortment of digging tools.

At the time of Monterey's mad scramble for gold, the property, located between the Walter Colton Elementary School (now the Monterey Peninsula Unified School District's offices) and Monterey High School, was owned by the Monterey School District. Excavations and preparations for the construction of a music building is what caused the unearthing of the first coins.

Even though the deed to the property carried a clause "reserving to the Martin estate all rights to buried treasure", the relatives of this late Montereyan did not attempt to claim any of the treasure that

Once the word was given, argonauts of all shapes and sizes went quickly to work. Note the pint-sized "gold digger" (third from right) with her king-sized rake. Credit — W.L. Morgan Collection — Monterey Public Library.

was found. Perhaps they felt they had "reaped the harvest" two years earlier when the stately old Martin mansion had been moved from its original location. . . , and the tidy sum of $1,500.00 was unearthed from the "rich" soil!

As the evening wore on and darkness came, gold hill took on the atmosphere of a happy community gathering. Huge bonfires lit up the sky and local residents happily wished each other luck as they trudged up the hill, burdened with shovels, lanterns and midnight snacks. During the long night several containers filled with twenty-dollar gold pieces were reported to have been found.

As the sun's early rays lit up the eastern sky, all-night stragglers could be seen slowly making their way down the hill, only to be greeted by curious newcomers and construction workers who were arriving on the scene.

Mike Maiorana, a lad of twelve, was one of these early morning arrivals. With a small rake in his hands, Mike was determined to find a fortune before school started that day. Heading for a spot where one of his friends had found a single gold coin, Mike fell to his knees and, with the first scratch of his rake, he exposed the upper portion of a long-buried can. Unfortunately, a sharp-eyed "prospector" standing nearby also spotted the can and rushed to Mike's side exclaiming, "What have you got there son?" Wise to the ways of the world, Mike tried to pass his find off as nothing more than a rusted can lid. Realizing what could be in the can, the excited gold seeker would have none of this, and, with a mighty swing of his pick, he split the can. . . revealing its contents. Seeing a stack of coins firmly held in place by the soil of gold hill, the impassioned argonaut dropped to his knees and wildly began scratching and clawing at the loose dirt!

A goodly crowd witnessed the excitement generated by this seeker of fortune and rushed to the scene of Monterey's latest strike. Mike managed to grab four of the top coins before he was picked up by the seat of his pants and thrown to the outer fringes of the mob. Staring in bewilderment at the gold-crazed crowd, Mike wisely stayed his distance as the eager prospectors fought with fists and shovels in their efforts to claim the newly-found treasure. Soon, realizing a group of outsiders were eyeing him coldly, Mike decided to settle for what he had, and made a quick exit from the scene. Clutching his four coins tightly in his hands, he raced down the hill to the safety of a nearby friend's house.

As Mike left the area, Nick Marazzo, the operator of a bulldozer at the school site, and a witness to the events leading up to the early morning scramble, made his presence known. Firing up his machine he headed straight for the coins! Only when this "iron monster" approached the strike, did the angry mob reluctantly vacate the site. Parking his "cat" squarely atop the coins Marazzo refused to move the bulldozer until the police were called and Mike had returned.

Mike Maiorana as he appeared twenty-five years after his fabulous find of 37 twenty-dollar gold pieces. The picture was taken at the site of Monterey's century-late rush for gold, and Mike holds one of the coins he found. Credit — R.A. Reinstedt Collection.

Soon the police had the area roped off and Mike had been summoned from his friend's hide-a-way. With the crowd safely behind ropes and Mike again on the scene, Marazzo backed his machine off the coins. With most of the gold still firmly held by the unyielding soil, Mike and a few workmen carefully removed the can and its valuable contents.

Counting out 37 twenty-dollar gold pieces, Mike's strike was the biggest single find. . . , up to that point. After generously handing out coins to the people who had helped him and, after being victimized by a "trusted" helper, Mike was escorted home by the Monterey police with less than half of the original 37 gold pieces.

When the news of Mike's find was reported in the evening paper, it is not difficult to imagine the mob scene gold hill was to experience during the long night ahead. People began arriving by the carloads and it was not long before there was scarcely a spot left to dig.

Young, old, doctors, lawyers, beggermen and thieves rubbed shoulders during that long January night. Mothers holding infants, housewives wielding kitchen utensils, grandmothers with garden trowels, and an astonishing collection of local canines, were all an active part of the frantic search for gold.

Only estimates have been made as to how much gold was found on that hectic 1948 night. No one knows for sure, as much of the money was quietly pocketed, fearing a scene similar to what young Mike Maiorana had experienced less than twenty-four hours before.

The following day Joe Duckworth, an off duty policeman, made what is thought to have been the biggest single strike. Surveying the activity, he spotted a glass jar that had been deposited almost at his feet by the blade of a passing bulldozer. After picking up the jar and seeing what it contained, Duckworth lined up the construction workers, a few friends who happened to be in the area, and a grandnephew of the late Will Martin who stepped from the crowd.

With a flourish few people have had the honor of witnessing, this generous Monterey policeman handed out coins until he had only a few remaining. Bystanders estimated that the jar that had been so conveniently deposited at this philanthropist's feet contained between forty and fifty twenty-dollar gold pieces!

With no important finds in the twenty-four hour period following the Duckworth find, interest in Monterey's century-late rush for gold began to wane. One by one the prospectors packed up their "diggin" tools and headed for home.

Even though Monterey's rush for gold was not without problems, today most old-timers remember it as being a time of fun, excitement, and much good-natured teasing. Back-slapping and socializing was the order of the day, and the added incentive of finding a fortune was only frosting on the cake.

How much gold was actually uncovered in this "Monterey Mother Lode" is open to question. Newspaper accounts estimated the haul to have been in the neighborhood of 400 twenty-dollar gold pieces.

Today a music building stands on the site of this lost bonanza. The name of the building, quite appropriately, is Treasure Music Hall — a modern monument to Monterey's century-late rush for gold.

Off duty policeman Joe Duckworth displays his jar of twenty-dollar gold pieces. Keeping only a few coins for himself, Duckworth shared his newly-found wealth with others at the construction site. Credit — W.L. Morgan Collection — Monterey Public Library.

AUTHOR'S NOTE

With the treasure section coming to an end, the author wishes to emphasize that tales of this type have a habit of becoming twisted and exaggerated, and that no guarantee can be made as to the amount of wealth involved, or to the locations where the treasures are hidden. It should also be mentioned that most of today's treasure sites are on private property and, before digging tools are dusted off and "witching sticks" are trimmed from nearby trees, permission should be gained from property owners as well as proper authorities before a treasure-seeking expedition is begun.

TALES OF
PIRATES
AND
ATTACKS FROM THE SEA

The harbor community of Monterey, historically important as California's first capital city, boasts an added measure of fame by being one of the few Pacific ports to have been visited — and sacked — by a pirate. Unlike numerous coastal communities along the Atlantic seaboard, where long-ago pirates made frequent sojourns, the history of the Pacific Coast is almost void of these boisterous buccaneers and their mutinous crews.

In searching aged documents and yellowed accounts of long-forgotten happenings, there are relatively few names that come to the front as the subject of Pacific Coast pirates is thoroughly researched. Two of the names that are most frequently mentioned are names that are historically linked to the colorful history of the Monterey Bay area. The first of these names and the story of this pirate's long ago visit to central California's rounded bay has, for many years, created considerable controversy among historians. Francis Drake is the man in question and, without a doubt, this famed English privateer is one of the best known "pirates" to have sailed the seven seas!

Taking command of his own ship at the tender age of twenty-two, Drake was encouraged by Queen Elizabeth (the first) to attack Spanish ships and seize their cargo. Operating primarily in the areas of the West Indies and the Caribbean, Drake's daring raids proved amazingly successful, and he soon became one of the best known of the Elizabethan sea captains. Roaming at will and raiding Spanish ships as well as coastal communities, Drake is credited with having played an important part in establishing England as master of the seas. Dearly loved by his countrymen, and knighted by his Queen for being the first Englishman to circumvent the globe, Drake in turn was judged a pirate of the worst kind by the people of Spain, and was tabbed with the nickname of "The Dragon".

It was during his world voyage of 1577-1580 that Drake is

53

credited with having brought his vessel to anchor near the southerly entrance of Monterey Bay. Returning to his ship after a visit to the Monterey shores, the GOLDEN HIND must have proved a memorable sight to Drake as, during his northerly voyage up the Pacific Coast, historians describe the luxuriantly-fitted vessel as having been "loaded almost to the sinking point with treasure"!

The treasure in question was the spoils of several Spanish galleons Drake had attacked, as well as the loot of communities he had sacked, on his voyage up the coast. Realizing his ship was in no condition to outrun or attack another Spanish vessel, Drake proceeded to make his way up the California coast in search of an inlet in which he could make much-needed repairs to his overloaded ship, and far enough north to avoid the ever increasing number of Spanish gunboats.

The rest of the story of Drake, England's magnificent sea dog, has often been told and is common knowledge to all who are fascinated with the exploits of pirates, explorers and long-ago adventurers. On June 17, 1579, records indicate Drake did find a bay suitable for the repair of his vessel. This harbor is generally accepted as Drake's Bay, located slightly north of world-famed San Francisco Bay. On July 23, 1579, with the repairs to the GOLDEN HIND completed, Drake pointed the bow of his ship toward the setting sun and continued his world voyage, eventually arriving to a hero's welcome in far-off England on November 3, 1580.

While in the San Francisco area Drake made friends with the Indians, conducted minor explorations and, of importance to this tale, left a plate of brass attached to a wooden post. Dated June 17, 1579, this historic brass plate had a message carved into it, and a silver sixpence piece attached to the lower right hand corner. The message read:

BEE IT KNOWNE VNTO ALL MEN BY THESE PRESENTS
IVNE 17, 1579
BY THE GRACE OF GOD AND IN THE NAME OF HERR
MAIESTY QVEEN ELIZABETH OF ENGLAND AND HERR
SVCCESSORS FOREVER I TAKE POSSESSION OF THIS
KINGDOME WHOSE KING AND PEOPLE FREELY RESIGNE
THEIR RIGHT AND TITLE IN THE WHOLE LAND VNTO
HERR
MAIESTIES KEEPEING NOW NAMED BY ME AN TO BEE
KNOWN VNTO ALL MEN AS NOVA ALBION
FRANCIS DRAKE

As fate would have it, the plate of brass left by Drake nearly four hundred years ago was found by a chauffeur near the shore of Drake's Bay in 1933. The small piece of metal (approximately 5 inches by 8 inches, by 1/8 inch thick), blackened with age, was thrown into the trunk of the chauffeur's car where it remained for many months. Eventually discarded near Point San Quentin (within the confines of San Francisco Bay), the small blackened plate was again picked up by a passerby in 1936. In the process of cleaning the aged metal, the new owner was amazed to discover that an elaborate message had once been painstakingly carved into the plate.

With much presence of mind, the finder took the metal with its mysterious message to the University of California. Here the relic was thoroughly cleaned, carefully inspected and scientifically studied. To the delight of historians throughout the world, the text of the message was officially made public on April 6, 1937.

With this valuable find serving as proof (to many) that Drake did visit the northern California shores nearly four centuries ago, it makes the story of Francis Drake's visitation to the Monterey area of even greater significance.

To get the full benefit of our story, we must go back to a crisp June day in 1934. On that long-ago day a distinguished Pebble Beach resident found an odd-shaped bottle half buried in the sand of the Monterey Peninsula's Moss Beach. Upon uncovering the antiquated container, the finder immediately realized his prize was not just another item washed ashore by the restless Pacific. Small barnacles clung to the bottle's crude moulding, and the brackish green of its original color had faded to a dull amethyst.

Packed with calcified sand and heavy with history, the discovery was taken home and used as a bookend for the succeeding fifteen years.

It was not until 1949 that the importance of the bottle and its valuable contents became known.

In the process of moving from one Peninsula location to another, tiny grains of the tightly packed sand began to filter out. With the sand beginning to trickle from the bottle, the owner decided to help nature along and began poking into the container in an attempt to empty all of the sand.

It was this probing into the aged hand-blown bottle that disclosed a small half-rounded object near the neck and, deeper inside, a slender metal cylinder.

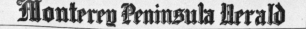

Monterey Peninsula Herald

MONTEREY, CALIFORNIA, WEDNESDAY, DECEMBER 7, 1949. 22 PAGES — SEVEN CENTS

Discovery Here Of Drake Scroll
May Change Pacific History

Gen. Groves Clears Hopkins, Wallace In Atom Investigation

WASHINGTON, Dec. 7 —Lt. Gen. Leslie R. Groves testified today that neither Harry Hopkins nor Henry A. Wallace ever tried to get any atomic secrets or materials from him for the Russians.

Groves, who headed the wartime atomic bomb project, told House investigators that he had never, in fact, met Hopkins or had any correspondence with him.

As for Wallace, Groves said the former Vice President never brought any direct pressure on him in connection with the atomic energy program, and, as far as he knows, never got on any indirect pressure.

Ask Report On Beach Purchase

San Francisco Drake Plate Found in 1937

The plate of brass (above) found near San Francisco in 1937 is believed to be that left by Sir Francis Drake when he landed there in 1579. First knowledge that Drake may have previously landed in Monterey is found in a lead tablet or scroll uncovered here only recently although actually discovered 11 years ago. Finder of the Monterey scroll refused to allow pictures of it, so the bottle in which it was contained, to be published until its authenticity is proven or disproven.

Check Authenticity Of Lead Tablet Found In Ancient Bottle

Seemingly Irrefutable Evidence That English Navigator Predated Viscaino

History of the Pacific Coast of North America was re-written today on a small lead tablet found on the Monterey Peninsula.

Seemingly irrefutable evidence has been found that Sir Francis Drake made his first landing on the Pacific Coast of what now is the United States near Monterey—not in the San Francisco Bay area.

The Herald has learned that a small lead plate carrying an exact description of a landing near Monterey by Drake and bearing his name and that of Francis Fletcher, his chaplain, was found some 11½ years ago at Far Shell Beach near the Monterey Peninsula Country Club.

Drake Story Is Too Big To Keep Secret

Shipments Legal To Russ in 1943, Says Acheson

WASHINGTON, Dec. 7 —Secretary of state Acheson said today that the Truman administration knew and approved of wartime atomic bomb material shipments to Russia in 1943.

San Francisco Drake Plaque Mentioned by Early Writers; Monterey Find Is A Surprise

The story of the recent discovery of a lead scroll purportedly left by Francis Drake on the Monterey Peninsula is told in adjoining columns of this page today.

San Francisco is the only other community beside Monterey, on the west coast of what is now the United States, that can claim concrete evidence that Sir Francis Drake visited the port, or immediate vicinity, during the voyage of 1579.

Last Minute News

BULLETIN !!!

Rites Mark 8th Anniversary Of Pearl Harbor

HONOLULU, T.H. Dec. 7 (UP) Only a solemn five-minute ceremony marked here today the eighth anniversary of the Japanese attack on Pearl Harbor.

Monterey Drake Scroll Checks With Known Historic Facts; Could Be Fake, But Clever One

Around World In Five Days

NEW YORK, Dec 7 —Two Los Angeles Jr. today finished wing-ing its way around the world in scheduled airline flights in 5 minutes less than five days.

Story of the Drake Bottle Is Intriguing, Dramatic Tale

In December of 1949, when the story of the Monterey Drake scroll became known, it was headline news in the Monterey Peninsula Herald. Credit — Lee Blaisdell photo — R.A. Reinstedt Collection.

Unable to extract either of the objects from the bottle, and not wanting to break the distinctive container, the owner took his find to a close friend for advice and help.

Myron Oliver, respected Peninsula resident, owner of a local art store and a qualified expert on antiques, studied the bottle with interest and recognized it as a beautiful and valuable find. With the aid of a pair of forceps he was able to delicately remove the smaller of the two objects.

Examination showed it to be a silver sixpence piece. The aged English coin had long ago been bent double, enabling it to fit through the neck of the bottle. The sixpence measured 1½ inches in diameter and showed the head of Queen Elizabeth on one side and her royal crest on the other.

Thrilled by the coin, the two friends pondered the problem of extracting the tightly-rolled cylinder from the bottle.

It took Oliver many attempts and over three hours of work before he was able to pull the mysterious metal roll through the narrow opening.

With the hammered lead cylinder finally free of its container, the men painstakingly tried to unroll it. They soon realized a message

The discovery of the above-pictured lead plaque serves as proof to many that Francis Drake visited the Monterey Bay area nearly four centuries ago. The above likeness is thought to be the only picture that exists of Monterey's mysterious Drake plate. Credit — R.A. Reinstedt Collection.

had been crudely engraved on the soft lead, but try as they might they were unable to keep the lead from curling.

Utilizing an old press (used to flatten prints, etc.), Oliver took a stack of blotter paper and carefully inserted the plaque between these papers. With the blotter paper acting as a cushion he gently began pressing the lead.

Successful in these efforts, the men were finally able to begin the task of deciphering the ancient message.

Within moments the excited pair realized the historical importance of the scroll. The crude lettering read:

> IN NOMINEE ELIZABETH HIBet BRITANNA
> RIARVM REGINA
> I DO CLAIM THIS GREAT LAND AND THE SEAS
> THEREOF, THERE BEING NO INHABITANTS IN
> POSSESSION TO WITNESS THERETO THIS BOTTLE
> AT GREAT TREE BY SMALL RIVER AT LAT. 36D.
> 30m. BEYOND HISP. FOVR OVR MOST FAIR AND
> PVISSANT QVEENE AND HERRE HEIRS AND SVCCESORS
> FOREVER VNTO THEIRR KEEPING.
> BY GOD'S GRACE THIS FIRST DAY OF MAY 1579
>
> FRANCIS DRAKE
> GENERALI
> FRANCIS FLETCHER
> Scriv

The plate measured 8 5/6 inches in length, 5 7/16 inches in width, and was approximately 1/32 of an inch thick. The latitude given was within minutes of the exact spot where the bottle was found. The May 1, 1579 date, predates the better known brass Drake plate of the San Francisco Bay area by one month and seventeen days.

In checking the particulars of Drake's world voyage, one must admit it is quite possible the famed English privateer landed on the Monterey shores before reaching the San Francisco area.

Drake is known to have left Guatulco, Mexico, in April of 1579, and arrived in the vicinity of San Francisco Bay on June 3rd of the same year. A Monterey landing on May 1st could, very possibly, have fit into that timetable.

The wording and spelling engraved on the scroll is of the type common to the English of the 1500s, and compares favorably with the wording of the brass Drake plate of the San Francisco Bay area.

The document bears the name of Francis Drake as well as Francis Fletcher, who was the chaplain and chronicler of the world voyage.

The bottle itself was taken to Boston where it was chemically analyzed. The results proved the glass to be the necessary 400 years of age.

With these facts to substantiate the story and give credibility to the plaque, the inevitable questions of "where is the scroll now?", "what has become of the bottle?", "why hasn't the discovery been made known?", and "who is the mysterious Monterey resident who made the find?", are repeatedly asked.

The answers to these questions are almost as amazing as the finding of the bottle itself.

Various efforts to have the scroll authenticated proved both frustrating and demoralizing. The outcome of the adverse publicity prompted the finder to insist that his name be kept anonymous.

Aside from having the bottle chemically analyzed and proven to be the necessary 400 years of age, the plate was sent to England where it was studied by a group of leading historians. Their final report indicated doubt as to the authenticity of the scroll — their reasoning stemming from their disbelief that the scroll had ever been rolled into a cylinder.

University officials at two leading California institutions examined the document and felt it to be authentic but, for reasons unknown to the owner, they refused to let their names or opinions be recorded.

If the aged lead plate is authentic, it is of interest to note that Francis Drake claimed "this great land" for England twenty-three years before Sebastian Vizcaino sailed into Monterey Bay and claimed the Alta California territory for the country of Spain. And, just for the record, Drake's landing on the California shores — whether it be Monterey or Drake's Bay — predates the Pilgrims' Atlantic landing at Plymouth Rock by forty-one years!

As to why the find hasn't been made known, the answer is — IT HAS! It was so "known" in 1949 that the finder reportedly rejected two offers of $5,000 and one offer of $7,500 for his story, the plaque and the bottle.

What has become of the plate and the 400-year old bottle is somewhat of a mystery. Rumors persist that it will "one day" become the property of the City of Monterey. However, if one believes the owner, this is almost an impossibility. During the latter part of 1965, while on a trip abroad, the finder of these valuable artifacts had his Monterey residence broken into, with many of his personal belongings stolen. Included in the lost bonanza was the lead plaque, as well as the coin and bottle!

While it is a fact that a robbery did take place, many old-timers in and around the Monterey Peninsula feel that the man who found the bottle was not the type to leave items of such historic significance lying about. They feel confident in their belief that the owner of the Drake-related items had secured them in a place where they could not have been stolen. They also feel that the story of their loss provided the finder with a convenient hedge, "to keep curiosity seekers and would-be historians away."*

Hopefully, one day the scroll will again be in the news – only this time it is hoped that the aged lead plaque will be accepted as conclusive evidence that Francis Drake, an Englishman, was the first European to have set foot on what eventually became the hub of Spain's far-reaching empire.

Out of respect for the Monterey Peninsula resident who found the aged bottle containing the Drake Plate, and in honoring his wish to remain anonymous, the name of the finder, and owner, of the Drake artifacts has purposely been ommitted from this narrative.

I n setting the stage for an account of Monterey's second encounter with a well-known pirate, as well as additional tales of California's capital city under attack from the sea, a brief glimpse into the history of Monterey and her rounded bay is in order.

It was on the 16th of December, 1602, that the previously-mentioned explorer Sebastian Vizcaino rounded the Point of Pines (Pacific Grove's Point Pinos) and discovered what he thought to be an ideal harbor for Spain's treasure-laden Manila galleons – similar to the vessels Drake had so successfully plundered twenty-three years before.

Being so enamored with the glistening blue waters and the white sandy beaches of the peaceful bay, Vizcaino bestowed the name El Puerto de Monte Rey upon his discovery, in honor of the Viceroy of New Spain, the Count de Monte Rey.

In a letter dated December 28, 1602, Vizcaino praised the harbor and described it and the surrounding territory as 'being secure against all winds, thickly peopled by Indians, very fertile, resembling Castile (Spain) in its climate and soil, boasting extensive lands fit for pasture', and, possibly most important of all, he stated:

> "Asto what this harbor of Monterey is, in addition to being so well situated in point of latitude for that which His Majesty intends to do for the protection and security of ships coming from the Philippines: In it may be repaired the damages which they have sustained, for there is a great extent of pine forest from which to obtain masts and yards, even though the vessel be of a thousand tons burthen, live oaks and white oaks for shipbuilding, and this close to the seaside in great number."

Father Antonio de la Ascension, who accompanied Vizcaino on this history-making voyage, also praised the rounded bay on California's upper coast, describing it in the following glowing terms:

> "It is a very good harbor and offers good protection and is sheltered from all winds. It has extensive forests and an infinite number of great pines, straight and smooth, fit for masts and spars of ships. Likewise evergreen oaks of a prodigious size proper for building ships."

As optimistic as these early accounts were, and as promising as the port of Monterey appeared to these visitors of so long ago, over the years Monterey Bay has proved to be anything but the peaceful Pacific paradise envisioned by these hearty explorers of yesteryear.

Pacific storms and ocean winds so frequently churned up the waters of Vizcaino's "sheltered harbor" that navigators who were to follow, as well as leaders of land expeditions, had great difficulty recognizing the bay of Monterey that he so glowingly described in his accounts of 1602.

But. . . , over the years it has not only been nature's storms that have stirred the waters of Monterey's historic bay. With Father Junipero Serra reaching the rounded bay in 1770, the community of Monterey that was built on its shores became the capital city of Spain's far-reaching empire. Remaining the capital under Spanish, Mexican and early United States rule, the harbor of Monterey became the scene of many dramas — some of which are discussed to this day with tongue in cheek and a twinkle in the eye.

Of interest to us in this chapter are incidents that took place in the years of 1818, 1842, and 1846. The first of these long-ago happenings involves the dreaded Pacific pirate Hippolyte Bouchard. Dropping anchor under the cover of darkness on November 20, 1818, Bouchard's arrival caused waves of excitement and storms of protest — rivaling any "war of the elements" produced by nature!

Early the following morning the suspicions of the local citizens were justified when the smaller of the two vessels opened fire on Monterey's ill-equipped fort, or El Castillo as it was called by the Spaniards. With the crash of guns, it became quite clear to all what the mysterious visitors had in mind.

Her shots being answered by a volley of cannon balls from shore, the larger of the two ships moved in and, under a flag of truce, sent the following message to shore:

"To the commandante of the port of Monterey.

Dear Sir: Since the King of Spain has declared 'bloody war' on the Americans who do not wish to exist under his dominion, these same Americans have to make defense by waging war on land and sea. They make war with all the seriousness of purpose and with all the rights of nations. Therefore, having crossed the Pacific Ocean to this coast, I now desire the surrender of your city with all the furniture and other belongings of the King. If you do not do so, the city will be reduced to cinders, and also the other surrounding villages. It is within my power to bring about this destruction. You may evade all the above spilling of blood by agreeing to my proposal. If so, I shall desist from what I say. Be good enough to reply to me as soon as possible. May God keep you many years.

Hippolyte de Bouchard

Argentina November 23, 1818"

Alta California's governor, Pablo Vincente Sola (whose headquarters were in Monterey), sent a defiant reply to the demands of this pirate. The text of this message is of interest only in light of the final outcome of this privateer's attack. Sola, considered an honorable and dedicated governor, left nothing to the imagination, as in a later document he stated:

"I replied, saying that its governor looked with due scorn upon all that the said communication contained; that the great monarch whom he served had confided to him its command to defend it and keep it under his rule; that if he should use force as threatened, I with mine would make him know the honor and firmness with which I would repel him, and that while there was a man alive in the province he could not succeed in his plan of taking possession, since all its inhabitants were faithful servants of the king, and would shed the last drop of blood in his service."

One must admire Sola's unyielding attitude, or perhaps his attempt at a colossal bluff, as he knew full well there was little hope of resisting this belligerent buccaneer and his army of evil men.

Upon learning of the governor's decision, Bouchard's reaction was to send a large number of men in several small boats (four of which carried small cannons) to a beach near Vizcaino's Point of Pines.

Governor Sola countered with a company of twenty-five men from the fort (under the leadership of Alferez Estrada) in an attempt to prevent the landing. But, with the odds being nearly fourteen to one against them, it is little wonder Estrada and his gallant band of soldiers had little success in repulsing the enemy.

As Bouchard's men marched on El Castillo, the few "dedicated" Montereyans who had not already left town (even before the first cannon was fired) were now heading inland, their belongings piled high in creaking carretas and strapped to the backs of an assortment of pack animals. Many of these early-day "servants of the king" did not look back until they reached the safety and comfort of the inland missions of San Juan Bautista and San Antonio.

Staging a fruitless defense at the walls of the fort, Sola and the beleaguered Spanish garrison soon beat a hasty retreat of their own, managing to spike the cannons and burn the powder before they left. In their scramble for safety, these noble defenders of Monterey's proud fort managed to take one "two-pounder", two boxes of powder, 6,000 musket cartridges and the provincial archives. Sola and his disarrayed crew retreated a distance of some twenty miles before finally making camp at Rancho del Rey – near the present-day city of Salinas.

While at Rancho del Rey, Sola and his men were joined by reinforcements from San Jose and San Francisco, but instead of attacking and attempting to drive off the invaders, the Californians decided it best to play it safe and observe from a distance.

Sentinels were placed to watch the foe, and with that mighty display of force the gallant Californians, who Sola defiantly declared would shed their last drop of blood for the king, sat back and watched the pirates as they proceeded to take what they wanted and burn what was left!

Hippolyte Bouchard (taken from a portrait of the famous Pacific pirate). Sailing under the flag of the "Republic of Buenos Aires", this fiery French privateer attacked and burned the capital city of Monterey in 1818. Credit — Colton Hall Collection.

After several days of plunder and pillage — taking livestock, robbing stores, destroying orchards, burning buildings, and drinking what "vino" they could lay their hands on — the fiery French pirate chieftain ordered his motley crew back to their ships.

On December 1st, after almost total destruction of the port city of Monterey and the Spanish stronghold on the hill, the dreaded pirate and his evil crew sailed, unmolested, from the bay.

It is of interest to note that Bouchard's appearance on the south side of Monterey Bay also had a profound effect on the people of Branciforte, located on the bay's north shore (where the city of Santa Cruz now stands). With the majority of residents fleeing to the safety of inland communities, as did the people of Monterey, a notable few of the more dedicated Branciforte citizens stayed just long enough to rescue valuables from Mission Santa Cruz. Unfortunately, many of these prized possessions — articles that were so "reverently" saved from the greedy hands of the pirates — never found their way back to the mission. As history now tells us, if these priceless possessions had been left in the church, they would have been safe, as Bouchard did not so much as pay a courtesy call to the bayside community of Branciforte.

In taking his leave of the rounded bay, Bouchard left California's capital city and her under-manned fort in ruins. Monterey's nightmarish encounter with this dreaded Pacific pirate and his La Frigata Negra (black frigate) was long remembered by the people of Alta California. The only fruitful outcome of this dark page in Monterey's history, was a half-hearted attempt at rebuilding and strengthening El Castillo — with thoughts of putting up a better defense if a future enemy should attack California's capital city.

To the whimsical delight of modern-day historians, the Alta Californian's chance to again "show their colors" came a short twenty-four years later. In the intervening two-dozen years Mexico successfully staged a revolution and won her independence from Spain. After 300 years of domination from across the seas, Mexico was now in control of the new world colonies. This affected California only slightly, and when the change was officially made the people of Monterey gathered together chanting and shouting, "Viva la Independencia Mexicana: Viva Emperador Augustin I" (Long Live the Mexican Independence: Long Live Emperor Augustin the First). With a fiesta atmosphere prevailing, guns, cannons and drums saluted the new government — accompanied by church services, feasting, and a grand ball that lasted far into the night.

As the years rolled on, the young country under The Stars and Stripes, known to us all as the United States of America, and her even younger neighbor to the south had their disagreements. In the 1840s these "friendly relations" took a turn for the worse.

As problems mounted, and with communications leaving much to be desired, Commodore Thomas ap Catesby Jones, Commander of the United States Squadron in the Pacific, was in a state of animated suspension. About all he was certain of were his instructions which, in the event of war, called for him to hasten to Alta California and take possession — before the British could do the same!

On September 2, 1842, Jones was anchored in the harbor of Callao, Peru, keeping a watchful eye on the British Rear Admiral Thomas and his small fleet of English warships. On September 3rd, after receiving "secret" orders from England, Thomas and three of his men-of-war sailed suddenly from the Peruvian harbor — their destination a mystery to the Americans.

At about the same time Jones received communications, prompting him to believe the United States and Mexico had gone to war. Thinking Thomas had received similar information and was heading for California, Jones hastily hoisted anchor and sailed for the northerly city of Monterey.

Commodore Jones' flagship, the UNITED STATES, and the sloop-of-war CYANE, made a straight run to this Pacific prize. Thinking he was racing the British fleet, and knowing the first to reach the capital city would, in all probability, be in a position to capture it, Jones spared neither man nor ship in his effort to beat the British to Monterey!

To his great relief, on October 19th, after rounding the Point of Pines, Jones saw that he was the first to reach the bay of Monterey. Capturing an unsuspecting Mexican vessel (the JOVEN GUIPUZCOANA) which was sailing out of the bay, the two American men-of-war (and their captured Mexican prize) cautiously entered the capital city harbor. With The Stars and Stripes waving, Jones anchored as close to El Castillo as safety would allow.

Summoning an officer from the American ship FAMA, which was lying at anchor in the Monterey harbor, Jones learned that this vessel had recently arrived from Honolulu — where rumors of war were current. The officer also reported that while in Monterey he had heard talk that England was about to take possession of the land.

These reports, along with signs of preparation for a defense evident on shore, plus the fact that no Americans from the town had come forth to greet them, and the added threat of Thomas (and his superior English force) rounding the Point of Pines at any moment — prompted Jones into taking immediate action!

At 4 p.m., October 19, 1842, Commodore Thomas ap Catesby Jones sent Captain James Armstrong, under a flag of truce, to the shore of Alta California's capital city — demanding a surrender to the United States of America.

The document was addressed to the Mexican governor and to the military and civil commandant of Monterey. They were given until 9 a.m. the following day to consider the demands. Governor Juan Bautista Alvarado went through the formalities of inquiring from the military commandante as to what the existing means of defense were. Captain Mariano Silva reported within the hour that the fortifications "were of no consequence, as everybody knows."

A sketch by William Meyers (a member of Commodore Jones' crew), illustrates the taking of Monterey's El Castillo by the troops of Commodore Thomas ap Catesby Jones. In the bay, with American flags flying, are the U.S. frigate UNITED STATES and the sloop of war CYANE. Credit — Bancroft Library Collection.

With this in mind, and after conferring with officials and leading citizens, a decision was made to surrender to the United States. Official documents were drawn up, terms were settled, and all arrangements were made.

At 11 a.m., on the 20th of October, 1842, Jones sent 150 marines and sailors to the Monterey shore under the direction of Commander Stribling. At this time the Mexican garrison occupying El Castillo marched out of the fort with "colors flying and music playing." Straight to the government house they marched, where, without a shot being fired, they gave up their weapons.

So. . . , as in 1818, Alta California's capital city again fell to invaders. The only difference was in weakening the will of the people as well as the defenses of the rebuilt and strengthened fort on the hill, the conquering heros of 1842 did not have to fire a single shot!

Unfortunately, this was not the last invasion the residents of this port city were forced to endure. As a matter of record, it was not even their last encounter with an invading force from the United States of America.

Only a few hours after his supremely successful conquest, Jones, in the company of Thomas Oliver Larkin (one of the most respected and influential United States citizens living in Alta California), was studying letters and papers found in the Mexican comisario's office. Upon reading these documents, which were of relatively recent dates when compared to the dispatches he had received while in the harbor of Callao, Peru, Jones realized a terrible mistake had been made. All "current" information pointed to the United States and Mexico as still being on friendly terms!

With profuse apologies, The Stars and Stripes were lowered, the Mexican flag was raised, salutes were extended all around, and the capital city of Alta California was once again under Mexican rule.

So ended the occupation of 1842. About all that can be said for this long-ago fiasco is that Monterey proved to be a prize easily obtained by any interested party. In the defense of Commodore Thomas ap Catesby Jones, no one can fault him for the mistake that was made. Even though he was temporarily relieved of his command to please officials of the Mexican Government (who were understandably indignant over his actions), Jones was exonerated of all blame, and in 1846 he was again given command of the Pacific Squadron (after California had officially become a part of the United States).

This sets the stage for a rather repetitious and somewhat

Commodore John Drake Sloat — Commander of the United States naval forces in the Pacific waters. It was Sloat who, on the 7th of July, 1846, officially raised the American flag over the Custom House in Monterey. With this act, 600,000 square miles of Mexican territory became a part of the United States of America. Credit — Colton Hall Collection.

anticlimactic conclusion. On July 7, 1846, for the third time in twenty-eight years, the weary residents of Monterey were to witness the familiar scene of their capital city being taken by an enemy force.

As with Commodore Jones' "rehearsal" less than four years before, Commodore John Drake Sloat of the United States Navy sent troops ashore and, without resistance, The Stars and Stripes were once again raised over Monterey — officially, and for the last time, bringing Monterey, Alta California, and 600,000 square miles of Mexican territory under American rule!

The raising of the American flag over Monterey's Custom House and the taking of the capital city by Commodore John Drake Sloat. The ships shown, left to right, are the U.S. sloop of war CYANE, the U.S. frigate SAVANNAH (which was also the flagship), and the U.S. sloop of war LEVANT. The illustration was made for Major Edwin A. Sherman, Secretary of the Sloat Monument Association. The Sloat monument, on the grounds of the Monterey Presidio and overlooking Monterey Bay, was dedicated on the fiftieth anniversary of Sloat's landing, July 7, 1896. Credit — California Historical Society Collection.

SUMMARY

"Tales, Treasures and Pirates of old Monterey" is in no way meant to serve as the final word on the various subjects discussed in this book. As time marches on, and as more and more people become absorbed in the fascinating history of the Monterey Bay area, additional stories will be recorded, and new tales of treasures and hidden riches will come to light. With new tales surfacing at a comparatively rapid pace, and with countless old tales being recounted by those 'in the know', the subject of treasures alone could easily fill a volume of substantial bulk. Included in this publication are only a selected number of treasure tales that the author feels best illustrate the varied stories, and treasures, that abound in this area.

For those who have been bitten by the treasure bug, and still crave clues to new and unfound Monterey area riches, they may do well by looking into the history of the lost "bandit village" of Pilarcitos, or perhaps they may wish to attempt to answer the question of what the mysterious treasure was that was removed from the eight-foot hole found near the Cachagua-Carmel Valley Road intersection in the late 1800s. If Monterey's south coast is where one thinks the action is, there is always Lost Valley. . . , waiting to be found. According to early tales, a lost mission mine is located in this valley. Swords of eighteenth century design, breastplates, aged Spanish coins, and skulls of white men (said to have been killed by an Indian uprising), have all reportedly been found at the Lost Valley site and, according to treasure seekers, these tales add considerable credence to this interesting story. Farther south, and near the Los Burros Mining District, is the Santa Lucia mountain stream of Willow Creek. Boasting a picnic area near its mouth, this south coast stream is also said to be in the area in which $50,000.00 in Spanish gold coins was once lost. Reports of weekend gold-seekers who claim to have found Spanish coins in the Willow Creek area certainly do little to discredit this tale. (A more detailed account of the Willow Creek treasure tale can be found in the previously mentioned book "Monterey's Mother Lode".) Also along the south coast trail (some say the inland mission trail) is rumored to be a jackaroo palm. If this long-lost tree happens to be found, and if the tree is near the base of a cliff, one would do well to wait until mid-afternoon, as when the sun begins to settle in the western sky the shadow of the palm is said to point directly to the shaft of a hidden mine. Closer to Monterey, where the Carmel-Monterey road now winds, legend states there was once a shaft that took road work crews three days to fill. Old-timers tell of this shaft having been on the Carmel side of the hill, and state it was where long-ago Indians mined large quantities of valuable gold ore. A second tale of mining in the Monterey hills dates from the early days of Alta California's Mexican period. Boasting silver instead of gold, this long-lost mine has lured treasure seekers into the forested hills of old Monterey for 150 years.

As illustrated in the brief accounts listed above (and on the preceding page), stories of the Monterey area's hidden wealth are limitless with, perhaps, the true treasures being in the legends themselves.

On the subject of pirates, the story of Hippolyte Bouchard and his sacking of California's capital city is, without a doubt, one of the most colorful and dramatic of all Pacific pirate tales. For those who wish more information on the deeds and misdeeds of Pacific pirates, they would do well to research the names of Thomas Cavendish, Bartholomew Sharp, Thomas Rogers, and a somewhat mysterious privateer known to historians as Captain Charpes (Charpes was believed to have been English, but he sailed under a French flag). Although not as well known as their Atlantic counterparts, nevertheless these Pacific buccaneers were successful in their trade. Interested primarily in Spain's fantastically rich Manila galleons, these privateers usually avoided plundering coastal communities. It is with this in mind, and because their long-ago escapades did not bring them to the shores of Monterey, that their stories are not included in this book.

As a closing statement, it is hoped by the author that "Tales, Treasures and Pirates of old Monterey" has provided enjoyment for the reader and, in its own way, has given the reader an insight into the color, the pageantry and the background that has made the history of California's first capital city the unique treasure that it, in itself, is.

The End